The
Fructose Cookbook

D1361674

by
Minuha Cannon

The
East Woods
Press

Library of Congress Cataloging in Publication Data

Cannon, Minuha, 1912-

    The fructose cookbook.

    Includes index.
    1.   Cookery (Fructose)   I.   Title.
TX819.F78C36   641.6'3'6   79-4902
ISBN 0-914788-18-3

Illustrations by Eloise Pope.
Photograph of Minuha Cannon courtesy of the Richmond **Independent-Gazette.**
Cover art by Ed Rollins.
Typography by Raven Type.
Printed in the United States of America by the Hunter Publishing Company.

East Woods Press Books
Fast & McMillan Publishers, Inc.
820 East Boulevard
Charlotte, NC 28203

Contents

Foreword

The beneficial aspects of fructose in human nutrition have been known for many years, but it is only recently that this natural sugar has become commercially available. In 1969 scientists in Finland developed a process for producing pure crystalline fructose at reasonable prices, and since then its consumption has steadily increased.

Fructose, also known as fruit sugar or levulose, is one of nature's most commonly occurring sugars. Fruits and berries, for example, are 35-40% fructose per dry weight. I would like here to summarize several unique properties which distinguish fructose from other sweeteners, such as sucrose (table sugar), sorbitol and the so-called "high fructose" corn syrups:

1. Pure crystalline fructose is roughly one-third sweeter than table sugar, so that less is required in most applications. Since all sugars have the same caloric content, **less fructose means fewer calories**.

2. Crystalline fructose is about three times as sweet as sorbitol. Again less means fewer calories.

3. Although "high fructose" corn syrups contain some fructose (30%) they also contain other, less sweet sugars, and are thus not as sweet as pure fructose.

4. The body's metabolism of fructose is rapid and less dependent on the presence of insulin than the metabolism of sucrose or high fructose corn syrup. Therefore, diabetics under adequate medical care can use crystalline fructose to some extent without adverse effects.

5. Fructose actually enhances many flavors.

6. Fructose is easily dissolved in water and withstands boiling and baking. And since it is hygroscopic (takes up moisture), it enhances the freshness of baked goods.

Bearing in mind these advantages, I was happy to learn of Minuha Cannon's successes using pure crystalline fructose in her kitchen. The delicious recipes show how readers can now—like nature, herself—use fructose as a sweetener and flavor enhancer. In addition to its obvious epicurean delights, this book is particularly beneficial to those who are on a diabetic diet and/or wish to restrict their caloric intake while retaining sweetness in their diets.

Veikko A. Koivisto, M.D.
Nutrition Consultant
New Haven, Connecticut

Preface

I am about to make an astonishing statement, so read closely. **Every living cell in the human body requires sugar.** This means that it is natural to have a sweet tooth and utterly unreasonable to feel guilty about it. Nevertheless, there is increasing evidence that excessive sugar is bad for us; and statistics prove that the per capita consumption of sugar in this country is excessive, no doubt about that.

Bearing in mind these facts, you can imagine my delight when my interest in good nutrition led me to discover fructose, the advantages of which Dr. Koivisto has described so ably in the preceding pages. However, when I began to experiment substituting fructose for sugar in my favorite recipes, my culinary ego received a serious blow.

My reputation as a cook began when, as a bride during the second world war, I adapted triumphantly to the challenge of shortages. After that I lived for many years in a country community far from a grocery store. Yet when unexpected company came, I could be depended upon to transform the food on my shelves into a presentable meal.

But any smugness I may have accumulated through past performances disappeared when I began to cook with fructose. My luck and inspiration appeared to have deserted me. In short, I had a high percentage of failures.

Since I am adamantly opposed to waste of any kind, especially food, I could not let this go on. I consulted my biochemist friend, Dr. Janis Young, who suggested that I call the Finn-Cal Sweetener Company. Robert Aherne, the president, generously put the resources of his staff at my disposal, and I received invaluable information regarding relative sweetness, best cooking temperatures and how to use fructose most effectively.

I found myself back in the groove. Friends and family were smacking their lips again. Once more my contributions to potluck suppers were among the first to disappear.

Requests for recipes began pouring in not only from friends and acquaintances, but also from strangers who were interested in the health benefits of fructose. Since I was already writing down so many recipes, the idea of composing a fructose cookbook followed quite logically. The function of this book is to supply convenient, healthful and good-tasting recipes for people who would like to avail themselves of the health advantages of fructose but who may have neither the time nor the inclination to experiment with foods as I do.

On the presumption that other people are quite a bit like me, my first thought was that this would be my **very own** cookbook, foods that I personally enjoy adapted to fructose cookery. Of course every recipe would be taste-tested for no other reason than that I simply like to feed people. However, because I was so full of what I was doing, word quickly got around. Friends and friendly neighbors began knocking at my door with delicious goodies in one hand and recipes in the other. The only reward they asked was that they be included in tasting sessions.

Fair enough? No, not really, for I feel deeply indebted to the many people who made writing this book an adventure in group activity rather than a lonely, sterile experience. To mention all the names would take a chapter in itself. I would especially like to thank Dr. Janis Young for her positive encouragement; Corneles Van Peski, French chef, whose recipe for Superb Bran Muffins is worth the price of this cookbook; Elizabeth Grant, who lives so conveniently across the street and is an honest taster, a gourmet cook in her own right, and a willing lender of everything from muffin tins to a teaspoon of this or that; and Robert Aherne for providing so many short cuts.

Now I would like to tell you some practical pointers about fructose which you will need to consider if you are going to cook with it. First of all, as Dr. Koivisto pointed out, it is hygroscopic, which is a fancy way of saying that it attracts moisture from the air. Therefore, **it must be stored in tightly covered containers**. If some should become a little damp, let's say in your sugar bowl, this does not particularly harm it other than that you must make allowances. Obviously, a teaspoon of fructose which is three-quarters fructose and one-quarter water is not going to be as sweet as a teaspoon of dry fructose, nor will it react the same way in recipes.

The fact that fructose is sweeter than ordinary sugar makes it convenient for people who are trying to lose weight since you don't use as much. Fructose satisfies the natural need for sugar without having the hunger-producing effects that ordinary sugar has for many people.

The recipes in this book take into account the fact that fructose is more reactive than ordinary sugar. Since it browns more quickly, oven temperatures tend to be lower. When used on top of the stove as in the preparation of syrups, pickling solutions, jams and jellies, it is important to stir and to use a low flame.

In compiling **The Fructose Cookbook**, I have mainly attempted to enhance the lives of its users by providing enjoyable as well as healthful recipes. Many of them reflect the fact that I grew up in a city that teemed with people from many countries, a truly international melting pot. But after all, isn't that what our country is? The happiest experiences of my youth came from sharing music, dances, literature, art and, not least of all, foods. The blintzes and borsht which were a commonplace to me were as exotic to my friend as her Austrian mother's sauerbraten were to me.

It must be just as evident that I am very interested in natural foods. Many of the recipes contain seeds, either ground or whole, whole grain flours, bran, yogurt, and carob powder instead of chocolate. Indeed, my interest in fructose is in itself an indication of my involvement with healthful nutrition.

You may wish to experiment, as I do, using your favorite ingredients. I often substitute small amounts of any of the following for an equal amount of flour in a recipe: ground sunflower seeds, rice polishings, bran, ground sesame seeds, ground almonds. In recipes calling for fresh fruits or vegetables, I substitute produce which is in season and therefore at its best as well as most economical. And don't be afraid to take advantage of accidents. One of my most delicious jars of pickled watermelon rind resulted from accidentally using a vanilla bean instead of a stick of cinnamon.

Each recipe in this book has been prepared in my kitchen exactly as described and taste-tested. However, you may wish to modify them according to your needs and tastes. I tend to use salt lightly. You may wish to add more, or you may wish to eliminate it altogether. The size of eggs makes a difference in some recipes. I use large eggs but have observed that even in the same carton sizes vary. If you are using smaller ones, you should either add an extra egg or reduce the amount of dry ingredients proportionally. The tartness of fruits varies, and the amount of sweetness people prefer varies. I have tried to take an average.

For me a recipe book is like traveling with a guide. He knows much more about his area than I have had time to find out, and I am very glad of his services. But it is fun sometimes to slip away on my own and see what I can discover. I urge you to do the same with fructose.

Beverages

Lemonade

¾ cup lemon juice
1 cup fructose
8 cups water

Stir and chill. The amount of fructose can be regulated to taste. This combines well with other fruit juices and adds a tangy flavor. It is also excellent in hot drinks such as herb teas.

9 8-oz. servings

Spiced Lemon Punch

1½ cups fructose
12 cups water, divided
1 stick cinnamon
8 whole cloves
8 whole allspice
1 cup lemon juice

Pour just 2 cups of water into a stainless kettle. Add the fructose and bring to a boil. Remove from the heat and add the spices. Allow to steep at least 2 hours. Strain into a pitcher and add 1 cup lemon juice and the remaining 10 cups of water, hot or cold as desired.

This is good served by itself or combined with other juices. It is especially good with tea or as a base for mulled wine.

18 6-oz. servings

Cranberry Juice

1 lb. cranberries
6 cups water
⅔ cup fructose

Bring cranberries and water to a boil in a large saucepan. Simmer until cranberries pop, about 5 minutes. Strain and return juice to saucepan. Add the fructose and bring to a boil. Remove from heat.

12 5-oz. servings

Spiced Cranberry Punch

4 cups cranberry juice
½ stick cinnamon
3 whole cloves
3 whole allspice
1 tbsp. lemon juice (optional)

Combine the first four ingredients in a saucepan. Bring to a boil and simmer for 5 minutes. Remove from heat and stir in lemon juice.

6 5-oz. servings

Spiced Tomato Juice

1 cup hot water
2 bouillon cubes
1 stick cinnamon
4 cloves
¼ tsp. coriander
5 tsps. fructose
4 cups tomato juice

Bring to a boil in a saucepan the first five ingredients. Simmer for three minutes. Add the fructose and tomato juice and bring once more to a boil. Serve hot.

While I do not recommend overindulgence in anything, the fact that fructose aids in the metabolism of alcohol makes this an excellent hangover remedy. But you don't have to have a hangover to enjoy this on a chilly day.

8 5-oz. servings

Basic Eggnog

6 eggs, separated
¼ cup fructose
2 tsps. vanilla
6 cups milk
nutmeg

Beat egg yolks and fructose until light colored. Stir in milk and vanilla (rum flavoring if desired). Beat egg whites until stiff but not dry. Fold into mixture. When serving, sprinkle a little nutmeg on top of each glass of eggnog.

12 5-oz. servings

Cranberry Eggnog

Add 3 cups of Cranberry Juice or Spiced Cranberry Punch to the above recipe.

16 5-oz. servings

Banana Eggnog

Prepare basic recipe using just 4 cups of milk. Place in a blender 3 medium bananas and 2 cups of milk. Blend until smooth. Stir thoroughly into the first mixture.

12 5-oz. servings

Fruit Juice Eggnog

Any of your favorite juices can be substituted for the cranberry juice in Cranberry Eggnog. If you use orange juice, try floating grated orange rind on top of the eggnog instead of nutmeg.

16 5-oz. servings

Buttermilk Eggnog

1 egg
2 tbsps. fructose
1 tbsp. lemon juice
¼ tsp. vanilla
1 cup buttermilk
1/8 tsp. nutmeg

Mix in a bowl or blender the first five ingredients. Pour into a tall glass and sprinkle with nutmeg. This is good hot or cold. Like the basic eggnog recipe, this may also be varied with fruit and fruit juices.

1 10-oz. serving

Peanut Butter Milk Shake

For each serving mix in blender or
mixing bowl:
1 tbsp. peanut butter
1 tsp. fructose
¾ cup milk

This is good served either hot or cold. If
you like, a dash of nutmeg may be sprinkled
on top or ½ tsp. grated orange rind.

1 8-oz. serving

Peanut Butter Eggnog

Blend or beat an egg into the above mixture. Add ½ tsp. vanilla.

1 8-oz. serving

Buttermilk Peanut Butter Shake

Substitute buttermilk for the milk in the
above recipe and add 1 tsp. fructose, a total
of 2 tsps. fructose for each serving. Egg may
also be added to this.

1 8-oz. serving

The Fructose Cookbook

Carob Meal-in-a-Glass

1 cup buttermilk
1 tbsp. fructose
1 egg
1 tbsp. carob powder
1 banana, cut in chunks

Place all of the ingredients in a blender and blend until smooth. I often add ¼ tsp. powdered magnesium oxide to this and a tablespoon of Brewer's Yeast or desiccated liver.

1 10-oz. serving

Grapefruit-Banana Quick Breakfast

For those times you've overslept and want something nourishing that you can sip on while you get dressed, add a cup of milk or buttermilk to the following recipe and another teaspoon of fructose. An egg can also be added beneficially.

1 12-oz. serving

Grapefruit-Banana Energizer

1 grapefruit
1 banana
1 tsp. fructose

Peel grapefruit, remove seeds and cut in chunks. Peel banana and slice. Place grapefruit and banana with fructose in a blender until smooth.

This recipe is so simple that it almost did not get included. It is one of my favorites for those times when my body and mind begin to get sluggish and I want to keep on working.

1 6-oz. serving

Coffee Liqueur

2⅔ cups fructose
½ cup instant espresso coffee
    (I use Salvador brand)
2 cups boiling water
1 vanilla bean
1 quart vodka

Blend fructose thoroughly with the powdered coffee. Add vanilla bean, cut into small pieces. Over this mixture pour the boiling water and stir until coffee and fructose are dissolved. Allow to cool before adding the vodka. Place in dark air tight bottles and store for one month before using.

40 servings

Soups

Dieters' Delight Oyster Stew

1 tsp. olive oil or other oil
¼ cup minced onions
1 clove garlic (optional)
1 10-oz. jar oysters
1 cup buttermilk
1 tbsp. fructose
1 tbsp. lemon juice
1 cup steamed cut-up greens

Heat the oil in the bottom of a saucepan. Add the minced onions and garlic and cook until golden. Add the oysters with liquid and bring to a boil. Add the rest of the ingredients and heat thoroughly once more. I like to use Chinese mustard greens in this recipe, but pick your own favorite. Spinach or collard greens are also very good.

In spite of its low calories, this stew has the advantage of staving off hunger for several hours.

2 servings

Scandinavian Dumplings

¼ cup flour
1 cup milk
½ tsp. salt
2 tsps. fructose
1/8 tsp. ground cardamom
2 tbsps. margarine or butter
1 beaten egg
2 tbsps. ground almonds
1 tbsp. minced parsley

In a saucepan make a paste of the flour and a small amount of the milk. Stir in the remaining milk, salt, fructose and cardamom. Cook over low heat stirring constantly until thick. Remove from heat and stir in butter or margarine until melted. Pour over the beaten egg and mix thoroughly. Let cool. Add almonds and parsley, stirring well. Drop by heaping teaspoons into simmering soup. Cook until dumplings rise to the top, about 2 to 3 minutes.

6 servings

Leftover Chicken or Turkey Soup with Dumplings

2 cups diced chicken or turkey
(ham, beef, etc.)
6 cups broth or bouillon

Bring liquid and meat to a boil. Reduce heat to simmer and add dumplings as described above. This is the time to use those drippings and juices I urge you to save.
6 servings

Borsht

Borsht is essentially a soup made of vegetables with or without meat to which is added lemon juice and a sweetener. My mother used honey or brown sugar. When the borsht was through cooking, she would taste it several times, adding either more lemon juice or sweetener after each tasting, while we waited impatiently. When she finally served it, we agreed that it was worth waiting for.

Cabbage Borsht

2 lbs. soup meat or beef brisket
1 medium sliced onion
2 cups tomatoes cut in chunks
8 cups water
3 cups shredded cabbage
½ cup raisins (optional)
Salt and pepper to taste
¼ cup lemon juice
2 tbsps. fructose or to taste

In a soup kettle place the meat, onion, tomatoes and water. Bring to a boil, cover and let simmer for 2 hours or until the meat is tender. Add the cabbage and raisins, if used, and simmer for another half hour or until the cabbage is tender. Add salt, pepper, lemon juice and fructose. Bring to a boil and simmer over very low heat for 5 minutes. Taste to adjust flavor. The meat may be cut up and served in the borsht or it may be removed and served as pot roast.

6 servings

Beet Borsht

1½ cups grated raw beets
2½ cups water
¼ cup lemon juice
2 tbsps. fructose or to taste (beets
vary in sweetness)
1 beaten egg (optional)

Place beets in a saucepan with water and bring to a boil. Simmer until tender. Add lemon juice and fructose. Bring just to boiling point and remove from heat. If used, stir egg in slowly.

If canned beets are used (No. 303 can), add enough water to juice to make 2½ cups of liquid. Bring beets and liquid to a boil, add lemon juice and fructose, heat again to boiling and remove from heat. Borsht is traditionally served with a gob of sour cream floating on it. Yogurt may be substituted. Sliced cucumbers and sliced green onions or chives may be added.

2 servings

Hearty Banana Soup

6 cups chicken stock
1 large potato
1 medium onion
2 tsps. soy sauce
½ tsp. curry powder
3 tbsps. lemon juice
½ cup peanut butter
2 tbsps. fructose
1 cup tomato juice
2 large bananas

Peel the potato and cut it into 1/8 inch slices. Cut onion into wedges. Place stock, potato, onion, soy sauce and curry powder in a large sauce pan. Bring to boil and simmer 10 minutes.

Blend lemon juice, peanut butter, fructose and tomato juice. Add to soup in saucepan. Bring to a boil. Peel and cut banana into 1/8 inch slices. Add to soup and simmer 3 minutes.

This Indonesian inspired recipe lends itself to variation. Beef stock or bouillon may be used instead of chicken stock. I sometimes add alfalfa sprouts along with the sliced bananas. ½ cup of Oriental rice threads may replace the potato. The addition of 2 cups leftover cubed meat makes this an ideal one-dish meal for a chilly day. Serve with hot rolls or your favorite crackers.

6 servings

Salads and Dressings

Mayonnaise

1 egg
1 tsp. prepared mustard
¾ tsp. salt
1 tsp. fructose
dash of tabasco sauce
3 tbsps. lemon juice or vinegar
1 cup salad oil

Mix thoroughly in a bowl or blender all of the ingredients except the salad oil. If using blender, add ¼ cup oil before blending. Then remove the cover insert and add the remainder of the oil steadily as the blender continues to operate. If using a bowl, add 1 tsp. of oil at a time, beating thoroughly after each addition, until you have used ½ cup. Then add 1 tbsp. at a time beating thoroughly after each addition until the entire amount is used up.

1 ¼ cups

Cucumber Dressing

¼ cup buttermilk
1 cucumber
1 tbsp. fructose
¼ tsp. salt
2 tbsps. cider vinegar
¼ tsp. crushed dill weed

Cut the cucumber into chunks. Place all of the ingredients in a blender and blend until the cucumber is cut up fine.

This tasty, low calorie dressing is good on many kinds of salad, such as cole slaw, salad greens, etc. It is especially good as a substitute for sour cream in Farmer's Chop Suey—that traditional combination of thinly sliced vegetables such as leeks, radishes and cucumbers.

1½ cups

Onion Dressing

⅔ cup cider vinegar
1 large onion, about ½ lb.
⅔ cup fructose
2 tsps. salt
1 tbsp. dry mustard
1 tsp. mustard seeds
2 cups salad oil

Slice the onion into chunks and put into a blender with vinegar. Blend for 30 seconds. Add the rest of the ingredients and blend until smooth.

This is a good all-around dressing, but it is especially tasty when used with fruits.

3½ cups

Fruited Coleslaw

4 cups grated cabbage
1 cup grated carrots
¾ cup crushed pineapple
2 cups diced fruit
½ cup mayonnaise
½ cup buttermilk
2 tbsps. fructose
2 tbsps. vinegar or lemon juice
½ tsp. salt

Combine the grated vegetables and diced fruits with crushed pineapple in a large bowl. For the diced fruits simply oranges and apples are delicious, but you may like to vary this according to your taste and what is in season. I sometimes cut a banana and avocado into this. Combine the remaining ingredients to make a dressing and stir well into the coleslaw.

10 servings

Jellied Vegetable Salad

3 tbsps. fructose
1 envelope gelatin
¼ tsp. salt
1¼ cups water, divided
¼ cup apple cider vinegar
1 medium-sized cucumber
2 cups grated carrots
¼ cup chopped celery
salad greens

Mix the gelatin, fructose and salt in a saucepan. Add ½ cup of the water and stir over low heat until gelatine is dissolved. Remove from heat and stir in the vinegar and the remaining ¾ cup water. Cut enough slices of cucumber to line a quart casserole. Chop the remaining cucumber. Pour a thin layer of the gelatin liquid over the bottom of the casserole. Place casserole and saucepan in the refrigerator until the gelatin liquid has the consistency of unbeaten egg white. Fold the grated carrots, chopped celery and chopped cucumber into the thickened liquid and pour over the cucumber slices in the casserole. Chill until firm and unmold on a bed of salad greens.

6 servings

Fruited Vegetable Salad

The above recipe may be varied by adding ½ cup fresh fruit of your choice, diced, or ½ cup of any of the following: canned crushed pineapple, drained; chopped dates; raisins.

6 servings

Festive Fruit Salad

Bottom Layer:
2 cups cranberries
½ cup water
½ cup fructose
1 cup fresh strawberries
1 envelope gelatin
1 tbsp. fructose
¼ tsp. salt
½ cup water
1 cup yogurt (or sour cream)

Second Layer:
1 envelope gelatin
1 tbsp. fructose
¼ tsp. salt
½ cup water
½ cup pineapple liquid
½ cup crushed pineapple
1 large avocado, mashed
1 mashed banana
1 tbsp. grated orange rind
1 orange, cut in chunks
¼ cup mayonnaise

Cook cranberries in water until cranberries pop. Add fructose and strawberries. Simmer 4 minutes. Combine gelatin, fructose and salt in a small saucepan. Add ½ cup water, stir over low heat until dissolved. Combine thoroughly with first mixture. Place in bottom of a 6-cup mold and chill. When firm, spread with yogurt.

Combine gelatin, fructose, salt and water. Heat as above. Add unsweetened pineapple liquid. Mix thoroughly with remaining ingredients. Spread over jelled layer and return to refrigerator until firm.

The visual appeal of this salad as well as its tastiness add up to an ideal accompaniment to a holiday feast.

10 servings

Salads and Dressings

Festive Fruit and Chicken Salad

For an outstanding hot weather main dish follow the Festive Fruit Salad recipe above substituting 1 cup seedless grapes for the orange in the second layer and adding a cup of diced cooked chicken.

4 servings

Festive Fruit and Turkey Salad

Follow the above method using turkey instead of chicken.

4 servings

Festive Fruit and Tuna Salad

Follow the method for Festive Fruit and Chicken Salad, but substitute ½ cup sliced green pepper instead of grapes and add a drained can of tuna fish.

4 servings

Chicken Mousse

1 envelope gelatin
½ cup water
1 cup chicken bouillon
1 tbsp. minced onion
3 tbsps. chopped celery
1 tbsp. chopped ripe olives
1 ½ cups diced cooked chicken
1 tbsp. fructose
2 tbsps. lemon juice
1 cup heavy cream, whipped

Place the water in a saucepan and sprinkle the gelatin over it. Cook over low heat until gelatin is dissolved. Remove from heat and stir in chicken bouillon. Chill in the refrigerator until it has the thickness of unbeaten egg whites. Add the rest of the ingredients, folding in the whipped cream last. Pour into a 4-cup mold and replace in refrigerator until firm. When ready to serve, unmold on serving dish. This is visually as well as nutritionally enhanced if you line the serving dish with lettuce or other greens.

4 servings

Low Calorie Chicken Mousse

Following the above recipe, save out the lemon juice and substitute whipped skim milk powder for the whipped cream. To make whipped skim milk powder, place ½ cup powdered milk in ½ cup ice-cold water. Whip until it forms soft peaks. Add the 2 tbsps. lemon juice and continue whipping until the peaks are firm. Fold into the gelatin mixture and chill and serve as described above.

4 servings

Chopped Herring Salad

1 cup chopped, pickled herring
½ cup chopped onions
2 hard-boiled eggs
1 apple, peeled and cored
1 slice bread soaked in herring liquid
1 tbsp. mayonnaise
1 tsp. fructose
Salt and pepper to taste

Chop together all of the ingredients and chill. The onions from the pickling of the herring can be used in this recipe instead of fresh onions. As a salad, serve on a bed of lettuce garnished with tomato slices and olives.

For hors d'oeuvres, spread on rounds of rye bread or crackers. Top with a thin slice of pimiento.

3 cups

Bread and Rolls

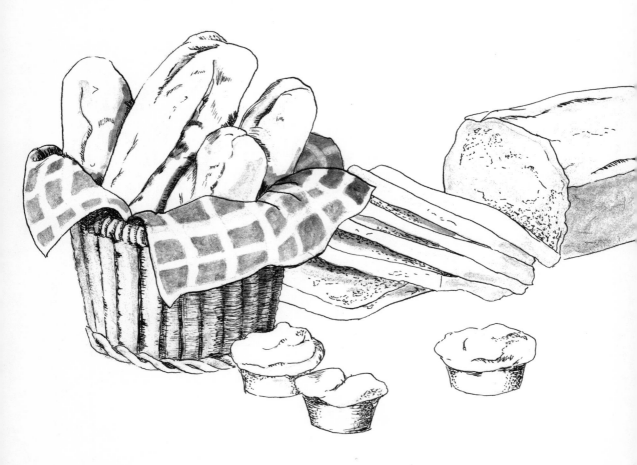

Wheat Bread

¼ cup fructose
1 tbsp. dry yeast (1 package)
⅓ cup lukewarm water
2 cups scalded milk
1 tbsp. salt
¼ cup butter or margarine
2 cups whole wheat flour
2½ cups white flour (about)

All ingredients should be at room temperature to start with. Combine the yeast with 1 tbsp. of the fructose and soften in the lukewarm water. (Be sure to use a container large enough to hold a cup and a half as this bubbles up.) Add the rest of the fructose, the salt and butter or margarine to the scalded milk and allow to cool to lukewarm. Add the yeast mixture and stir. Add the combined flours and mix well. Turn out on a floured board and knead thoroughly. Place in an oiled bowl. Brush the top with oil and cover. Let set in a warm place away from drafts until doubled in bulk. Punch down and knead again. Divide in two and form into loaves. Bake in greased tins. Preheat oven to 400 degrees and reduce temperature to 375 after putting loaves in oven. Bake for 50 minutes. Test for doneness by tapping bottom of loaf. It should have a hollow sound.

2 loaves, 16 slices each

Rye-Potato Bread

1 tbsp. fructose
1 tbsp. dry yeast
½ cup lukewarm water
2 tsps. salt
1 cup mashed potatoes
2 cups warm water
8 cups rye flour

Dissolve fructose and yeast in ½ cup warm water and let set for 5 minutes. Combine with 2 cups of warm water and salt. Add mashed potatoes and rye flour stirring well to make a soft, somewhat sticky dough. Knead until dough is smooth and holds its shape. Expect to use plenty of flour on your hands while kneading. If you add too much flour before kneading, the dough will be too heavy. Let rise until double in bulk in a warm place, covering bowl with a warm, damp cloth. Punch down and shape into 3 loaves. Place in greased 8½ x 4½ x 2½-inch loaf tins. Brush tops with oil and place in a warm place until loaves have doubled. Bake at 350 degrees for one hour.

This makes a substantial "sink your teeth into" bread, wonderful with melted cheese or Welsh rarebit. It is also excellent to serve to allergic friends as it contains no milk, wheat or eggs.

3 loaves, 16 slices each

Herbal-Tea Onion Bread

1 tbsp. herbal tea
2 cups boiling water
¼ cup margarine or butter
3 tbsps. fructose
2 tsps. salt
1 cup minced onion
½ cup warm water
1 tbsp. dry yeast
1 beaten egg
7 cups
   unbleached white flour

This is the recipe for you if you enjoy exotic flavors and also like to mystify your friends, who will beg to know the secret ingredient. If you wish, you may combine teas. I have used linden, chamomile, lemon grass and hops tea, usually singly.

Pour boiling water over the herbal tea. (A tea ball is useful.) Let steep for a half hour or more. Remove the tea. Add margarine or butter and heat just until margarine melts. Remove from heat. Add just two tbsps. of the fructose and the salt and onion. Cool to lukewarm. Dissolve yeast and remaining tbsp. of fructose in ½ cup warm water. Let stand 5 minutes. Add along with the beaten egg stirring into the lukewarm mixture. Beat in enough flour, one cup at a time, to make a smooth, soft dough. Turn out onto a floured board and knead until glossy. Place dough in a well-greased bowl and brush top with oil. Cover with a cloth dampened with warm water and let rise in a warm place until doubled. Punch down and shape into 3 small or 2 large loaves. Brush with oil and let rise again. until doubled. Bake at 375 degrees until the crust is golden and the loaves sound hollow when tapped, about one hour.

3 loaves, 16 slices each

Highland Shtetl Bread

2 tbsps. fructose
2 tbsps. dry yeast
½ cup lukewarm water
1 ½ cups boiled water
2 tsps. salt
1 cup quick-cooking oatmeal
6 cups flour
3 eggs
6 tablespoons shortening

Mix 1 tbsp. fructose with yeast and soften in the lukewarm water. Add the other tablespoon of fructose, the salt and the shortening to the hot water and allow to cool to lukewarm. Beat the eggs, reserving one yolk, into this liquid. Add the oatmeal and enough flour to make a soft but firm dough. (The size of the eggs will make some difference in the amount of flour.) Turn onto a well-floured board and knead until smooth and shiny. Place in a greased bowl. Brush the top with oil, cover and allow to rise until double in bulk. Punch down and knead again. Divide into 9 parts, shaping each part into a rope about one foot long. Press 3 of these together at one end and braid. Press together at the other end and place in a greased loaf tin. Braid two more loaves to make 3 loaves altogether. Mix the reserved egg yolk with 1 tbsp. cold water and, using a pastry brush, brush the tops of the loaves. These can be sprinkled with either poppy seed or sesame seed. Allow to rise again until double in bulk. Bake at 375 degrees about 1 hour until golden brown and sounding hollow when tapped.

3 loaves, 16 slices each

Swedish Rye-Cheese Pinwheels

1 cup scalded milk
2 tbsps. fructose
2 tsps. salt
3 tbsps. margarine or butter

½ cup water, lukewarm
1 package dry yeast
1 tbsp. fructose
1 beaten egg

2 cups rye flour
2 cups white,
    unbleached flour
2 cups
    grated yellow cheese

Using a large saucepan, stir the fructose, salt and margarine into the scalded milk. Let cool to lukewarm.

Meanwhile, dissolve the yeast and fructose in the water allowing to set 5 minutes. Stir into saucepan. Stir in the egg.

Combine the flours and beat into the mixture in saucepan. This should make a dough soft but firm enough to handle.

Turn the dough out onto a well-floured board and knead until it is smooth and shiny, at least five minutes. Place into a greased bowl, brush the top with oil, cover with a cloth and set in a warm place until it is doubled in bulk. Punch the dough down and divide it into six portions. Roll one portion out into an oblong approximately 4 by 10 inches. Spread with ⅓ cup grated cheese. Roll up jelly-roll fashion, brushing the edge with a little water to make a better seal. Cut into ½-inch slices, place on well-greased cookie tin, brush tops with oil and set in a warm place until double in bulk. Repeat with the remaining 5 portions of dough. Bake at 375 degrees until lightly browned, about 25 or 30 minutes.

120 pinwheels

Whole Wheat-Bran Muffins

2 cups whole wheat flour
1 ½ cups bran
¼ cup fructose
½ tsp. salt
1 ¼ tsp. soda
1 egg
¼ cup water
2 tbsps. melted butter or margarine
2 cups buttermilk
1 cup raisins

Mix the whole wheat flour, bran, fructose, salt and soda. In a large bowl beat up the egg, water, buttermilk and melted margarine or butter. Stir in the dry ingredients and raisins just enough to moisten. Bake in buttered muffin tins at 325 degrees for 40 minutes.

20 muffins

Bran-ana Muffins

1 cup unbleached white flour
1 cup bran
1 tsp. baking soda
¼ tsp. salt
1 egg, beaten
2 tbsps. margarine or butter
3 tbsps. fructose
3 tbsps. sour milk
2 medium bananas, mashed

Mix thoroughly together the flour, bran, baking soda and salt. Cream the margarine and fructose together. Beat well with the egg, bananas and sour milk. Pour in the dry ingredients and stir just until they are moistened. Fill greased and floured muffin tins half full. Bake in 350 degrees oven until lightly browned and toothpick comes out clean, about 40 minutes.

10 muffins

Chef Corneles Van Peski's
Superb Bran Muffins

1 cake compressed yeast
¼ cup lukewarm water
2 tbsps. fructose
1 cup lukewarm buttermilk
1/3 cup vegetable oil
2 beaten eggs
1 cup unbleached white flour
½ cup whole wheat flour
½ cup bran
2 tsps. baking powder
1 tsp. salt
1½ tsps. cinnamon
½ tsp. ginger
½ tsp. ground cloves
½ cup ground sunflower seeds
½ cup unsweetened grated coconut
½ cup toasted wheat germ
½ cup raisins
½ cup
   chopped dried apricots
1 cup
   toasted sunflower seeds
¾ cup grated carrots

Since Corneles Van Peski himself worked with fructose, this is the only contributed recipe I have not altered or adapted.

Dissolve yeast in lukewarm water. Add the fructose, buttermilk, vegetable oil and eggs, stirring thoroughly. Combine the white flour, whole wheat flour, bran, baking powder, salt, cinnamon, ginger and cloves. Beat into the first mixture ½ cup at a time. Stir the remaining ingredients together in a bowl and add to the first two combined mixtures. Beat just until these last ingredients are moistened. Cover, set in a warm place and allow to rise about ½ hour. Have muffin tins greased and hot. Spoon the mixture into the muffin cups so that they are about ¾ full. Bake at 375 degrees 15 to 20 minutes.

20 muffins

Yogurt Rolls

½ cup warm water
1 tbsp. dry yeast
⅓ cup fructose
1 cup yogurt
½ cup margarine or butter
2 eggs
1 tsp. salt
5½ cups flour, about

In a large mixing bowl dissolve the yeast and 2 tbsps. of the fructose in the warm water. Melt margarine or butter and allow to cool to lukewarm. Add yogurt, beaten egg and margarine or butter to the mixing bowl and stir thoroughly. Combine the salt, remaining fructose and flour. Add this mixture to the mixing bowl, about one third at a time beating thoroughly. This should make a soft, slightly sticky dough. The amount of flour depends on the size of the eggs. Turn out onto a well-floured board and knead for about 5 minutes. Place in a greased bowl, cover with a damp cloth and let rise in a warm place until doubled. Punch down. Put enough dough in muffin tins to fill them ⅓ full. Let rise to top of tins. Bake at 375 degrees about twenty minutes until golden brown.

These can also be shaped into your favorite forms, such as cloverleaf, bowknot, parker house rolls, etc.

24 rolls

Rice Flour Muffins

2 tbsps. margarine or butter
1 cup rice flour
1 tbsp. fructose
½ tsp. salt
2 tsps. baking powder
1 cup milk
1 beaten egg
¼ cup chopped raisins

Melt margarine. Mix the rice flour, fructose, salt and baking powder thoroughly. Stir together milk, egg and lukewarm margarine or butter. Pour into dry ingredients and mix just long enough to moisten them. Fold in chopped raisins. Do not over-mix. Bake in greased and floured muffin tins at 350 degrees for 25 minutes.

You don't have to be allergic to wheat to enjoy these muffins, but if you are, be sure to flour the muffin tins with rice flour. Serve hot with butter and/or marmalade or just plain.

12 muffins

Oatmeal Rolls

½ cup quick-cooking oatmeal
1 tbsp. butter or margarine
¼ tsp. salt
2 tbsps. fructose
1 cup boiling water
1 package (1 tbsp.) dry yeast
¼ cup warm water
2½ cups sifted flour

Place oatmeal, butter, salt and 1 tbsp. fructose in boiling water and bring to a second boil. Remove from heat immediately and cool to lukewarm. Dissolve the yeast and remaining tbsp. fructose in ¼ cup warm water. Stir into oatmeal mixture. Add enough flour to make a dough that can be handled but not too stiff. Knead thoroughly until dough is smooth and shiny. Place in a greased bowl, brush the top with oil, cover and let rise in a warm place until doubled in bulk. Punch down. Using a rounded tablespoon, place pieces of dough in well-greased muffin tins to a height of ½ inch. Brush the tops with oil and let rise again until doubled. Bake at 375 degrees for 25 to 35 minutes until a light golden brown.

This dough will adapt itself well to your favorite shapes of rolls, such as cloverleaf, parker house and bowknot.

15 rolls

Vegetables

Pickled Beets

½ cup beet liquid
1 cup vinegar
¼ cup fructose
5 whole cloves
5 whole allspice
½ tsp. cinnamon
1 bay leaf
1½ cups cooked beets, sliced or shredded

Place the first seven ingredients in a saucepan, using the liquid in which you have cooked the beets or, if using canned beets, liquid from the can. Bring to a boil and simmer 5 minutes. Place beets in a sterlized jar and cover with contents of saucepan. Screw lid over jar and let stand at least 24 hours before serving.

These beets are very good in salads or as a side dish. I like to use the juice with olive oil as a salad dressing.

6 servings

Broccoli, Dutch Style

4 cups broccoli, cut up
2 cups water
2 tbsps. margarine or butter
2 tbsps. flour
1 cup broccoli liquid
½ tsp. salt
¼ tsp. pepper (optional)
5 cloves
3 tbsps. vinegar
2 tbsps. fructose

Cook broccoli in 2 cups water until tender but firm. Drain, saving the liquid. Melt the margarine or butter in a stainless saucepan over low heat. Stir in the flour and cook till bubbly. Add gradually one cup of the reserved broccoli liquid and, stirring constantly, simmer until thick and smooth. Stir in the remaining ingredients and heat thoroughly. Pour over broccoli in a serving dish and toss until broccoli is evenly coated.

This recipe may be used substituting other vegetables such as zucchini, spinach, string beans, carrots, etc.

4 servings

Sweet and Sour Cabbage

4 cups shredded cabbage
1 cup sliced apple
1 cup boiling water
4 tsps. fructose
2 tbsps. vinegar or lemon juice
1 tsp. mixed whole spices
½ tsp. salt
pepper to taste

In a greased casserole place the cabbage and apples in layers. Tying the spices in cheese cloth or putting them in a tea caddy, combine the remaining ingredients and bring to a boil. Let steep for 10 minutes. Remove spices and pour the liquid over the casserole. Bake at 375 degrees until cabbage is tender. The ingredients may also be combined in a heavy saucepan and simmered until tender.

4 servings

Lemon-Glazed Carrots

1 cup carrot strips
2 tbsps. fructose
2 tbsps. lemon juice
2 tbsps. water
1 tbsp. margarine or butter

Steam carrot strips for 5 minutes. Combine fructose, lemon juice, water and margarine in a heavy 8-inch skillet. Bring to a boil and spread carrots evenly in the skillet. Simmer uncovered turning the carrots from time to time until most of the liquid has evaporated and the carrots are shiny.

2 servings

Orange-Glazed Carrots

In the above recipe use 4 tbsps. orange juice instead of the lemon juice and water and proceed as directed.

2 servings

Ginger-Glazed Carrots

Add a half-teaspoon of ginger to the glazing liquid in either of the above recipes.

2 servings

Zesty Carrots

2 tbsps. butter or margarine
1 cup chopped onions
½ cup boiling water
4 cups grated carrots
1 tbsp. fructose
½ tsp. salt

In a large pan soften onions in butter over a low flame. Stir in the remaining ingredients, cover closely and simmer for 10 minutes over low heat. Stir 2 or 3 times during cooking.

This makes an excellent side dish for dinner. I always make some extra so that I can have Eggs in a Golden Nest for the next day's lunch.

4 servings

Marinated Cucumber Spears

1 quart cucumber spears
1 cup vinegar
1 ¼ cups water
¼ cup fructose
1 ½ tsps. salt
1 tsp. pickling spices (or spices of
your choice)

Wash cucumbers, trim and cut into ½-inch wide spears. Fit into a 1-quart jar. Place the remaining ingredients into a saucepan and bring to a boil. Pour over the cucumbers. Let marinate at least 6 hours.

These are good served with sour cream, buttermilk or yogurt. They can also be used to pep up a salad.

6 servings

Vegetables Baked in Lemon-Buttermilk Sauce

2 cups vegetables, thinly sliced
½ cup buttermilk
1 egg
½ tsp. salt
2 tbsps. lemon juice
2 tbsps. fructose
1 tbsp. flour
1 tsp. cinnamon

Vegetables with relatively high moisture content, such as zucchini, tomatoes, egg-plant and onion, can be used directly. Root vegetables, such as turnips, carrots and beets, should be steamed for 10 minutes. This recipe adapts to the use of a single vegetable, (zucchini is one of my favorites), or any combination that suits your taste. Slice the vegetables very thin and place in a but-tered 9-inch baking dish. Beat together the next 6 ingredients and pour over the vegetables. Sprinkle cinnamon on the top. Bake at 350 degrees until set, about 20 minutes.

4 servings

Yams Baked in Cranberry-Pineapple Sauce

3 cups sliced cooked yams
1 tbsp. margarine or butter
½ cup Cranberry Sauce
⅓ cup crushed pineapple, unsweetened
2 tbsps. pineapple juice
1 tbsp. fructose
½ tsp. cinnamon
¼ tsp. salt
¼ cup sliced almonds

Combine all the ingredients except the yams and almonds in a saucepan and heat just until margarine is melted. In a buttered one-quart casserole place ⅓ of the yams. Over this spread ⅓ of the heated mixture. Repeat, making 3 layers in all. Sprinkle the almonds over the top. Bake at 350 degrees for 30 to 40 minutes.

4-6 servings

Main Courses

Roast Chicken in Simple Sauce

1 tbsp. fructose
1 tbsp. soy sauce
½ cup fruit or vegetable juice
½ tsp. ginger (optional)
1 chicken (3 lbs.)

In a baking dish large enough to hold your chicken combine the fructose, soy sauce and juice of your choice. (The juices I use most often are tomato, pineapple or orange. If you wish to use lemon juice, use only ¼ cup and add another ¼ cup of other juice, broth or water.) Turn the chicken in the sauce so that it is evenly coated inside and out. Bake at 400 degrees covered, breast side down, for 30 minutes. Turn heat down to 375 degrees, remove cover and turn chicken so that the breast is up. Bake until nicely browned, basting occasionally.

4-6 servings

Zesty Chicken with Orange-Almond Sauce

1 3-lb. frying chicken, cut up in serving pieces
1 tbsp. olive oil, or other oil
½ cup sliced onion
3 tbsps. flour
1 tsp. cinnamon
½ tsp. allspice
¼ tsp. nutmeg
1 tbsp. fructose
1 cup orange juice
1 tbsp. cider vinegar
2 tbsps. soy sauce
4 to 8 drops tabasco sauce (to taste)
1 orange, peeled and sliced
½ cup slivered almonds

Sauté onions in oil until soft. Set aside. Brown chicken in same pan. Remove pieces and set aside. Add flour and spices to drippings and stir until smooth. Combine fructose, orange juice, vinegar, soy sauce and tabasco. Stir into flour and drippings and heat until mixture comes to a boil. Add chicken and onions. Cover and cook over low heat until chicken is tender, turning occasionally, about 30-40 minutes. Add orange slices and almonds, and cook for 5 more minutes.

After adding the chicken and onions to the sauce, this could also be ovenbaked at 375 degrees for 40-60 minutes.

4-6 servings

61

Mediterranean Chicken

½ cup yogurt
2 tbsps. fructose
1 tsp. salt
2 tbsps. lemon juice
1 clove garlic minced
1 tsp. ground ginger
1/8 tsp. ground cardamon
1 tsp. ground coriander
1 frying chicken, cut up (about 3 lbs.)

Mix first 8 ingredients in a glass or stainless baking dish. Add chicken pieces, spooning mixture over chicken to coat pieces evenly. Let stand in refrigerator at least 3 hours. Set oven at 350 degrees. Bake covered for 45 minutes and uncovered for an additional 30 minutes.

The sauce must not be wasted! This is good over rice, or just sopped up with your favorite bread.

4-6 servings

Curried Chicken in Lemon Sauce

2 tbsps. margarine or butter
2 tbsps. chopped onion
2 tbsps. flour
¼ tsp. curry powder
salt and pepper to taste
1 cup milk
1 tbsp. fructose
2 tbsps. lemon juice
1 tbsp. grated lemon rind
1 ½ cups diced chicken, cooked

Heat the margarine and onion in a small saucepan over low heat until the onion is golden. Stir in the flour and seasonings. Add the milk slowly, stirring constantly. Cook until mixture thickens and stir in the fructose and lemon juice and rind. Add chicken. Continue to stir over low heat until mixture bubbles.

This is good served over rice, noodles or toast. Diced cooked turkey or ham may be substituted for the chicken.

4 servings

California Turkey Wings

2 lbs. turkey wings (about 2)
2 small lemons
⅓ cup rice polishings
½ tsp. salt
¼ tsp. white pepper
¼ tsp. paprika
1 chicken bouillon cube
4 tsps. fructose
1 cup hot water
3 tbsps. vegetable oil

Sprinkle the juice of one lemon over the turkey wings. Grate the rind of the lemon from which the juice was extracted. Slice the other lemon thinly and put slices aside. Mix the rice polishings, salt, pepper and paprika in a paper bag. Shake turkey wings in this mixture and brown them slowly in hot oil. Remove from flame and sprinkle with the grated lemon rind. Dissolve bouillon cube and fructose in hot water. Pour over the turkey wings. Distribute lemon slices evenly over the turkey wings. Cover and bake at 350 degrees for 1 hour.

4 servings

Turkey Lemon Soup

The juices from California Turkey Wings must be saved for a wonderful lemon-flavored soup made by adding water to your taste. Excellent with rice or Swedish dumplings added.

4 servings

Veal Kidneys Supreme

1 lb. veal kidneys
½ cup diced tomatoes
¼ cup green pepper, sliced
¼ cup minced onion
1 tbsp. fructose
¼ cup lemon juice
salt and pepper to taste

Soak kidneys in cold salt water for at least an hour. Rinse several times and drain. Slice lengthwise in half and remove most of the fat and gristle. Place all of the ingredients in a frying pan and simmer for 15 minutes.

2-3 servings

Veal Stew in Buttermilk Sauce

1 lb. boneless veal stew meat
½ cup sliced mushrooms
½ cup sliced onions
½ cup sliced green peppers
2 tbsps. oil
⅔ cup buttermilk
2 tbsps. fructose apricot-lime marmalade (or 1 tbsp. fructose, 1 tbsp. lime juice and 4 apricots, seeded and sliced)
1 tbsp. soy sauce, more or less to suit taste

Brown the veal in an iron or stainless frying pan at medium heat, using olive or peanut oil preferably. Add mushrooms, onions and green peppers and saute at low heat for five minutes. Stir marmalade and soy sauce into buttermilk and pour into the frying pan. Cover and bake in oven at 325 degrees for 1½ hours or until the veal is tender. Pineapple or other jams made with fructose may be used in place of the apricot jam.

2-3 servings

Sauerbraten

3 lbs. beef, chuck or rump
1 large clove garlic, cut
1 tsp. salt
½ tsp. pepper
2 cups vinegar
2 cups water
2 bay leaves
1 tsp. peppercorns
4 cloves
¼ cup fructose
2 tbsps. vegetable oil
½ cup sliced onion
1 cup carrots (cut in strips if desired)
cornstarch
⅓ cup Ginger-Carob Thin crumbs
1 cup yogurt

Rub the beef on all sides with the cut surface of the garlic. Place in a deep bowl. Heat together the salt, pepper, vinegar, water, bay leaves, peppercorn, cloves and fructose. Bring just to boiling and pour over the beef. Let stand in refrigerator for 4 days. Turn the meat each day. Heat 2 tbsps. oil in a deep skillet, preferably iron. Remove meat from the bowl and brown in the skillet on all sides. Add the onion slices and, if you wish, the carrot strips. Strain the liquid from the bowl in which the meat was soaking and pour it over the meat and vegetables in the skillet. Cover and bake at 300 degrees for 3 hours or until meat is tender.

To make gravy remove meat and vegetables from the skillet. Add to the liquid 1 tbsp. cornstarch for each cup of liquid. Cook, stirring constantly, until gravy is smooth. Stir in the ginger-carob cookie crumbs and yogurt and pour over the meat in a serving dish.

6-8 servings

Stuffed Green Peppers with Tomato Sauce

6 green peppers
1 lb. ground chuck
1 cup cooked brown rice
1 clove garlic, minced
¼ cup onion, minced
1 egg
1 tbsp. parsley flakes
½ tsp. salt
1 tsp. ground thyme
1 cup tomato sauce
½ cup hot water
1 tbsp. fructose
3 tbsps. vinegar

Prepare green pepper shells: slice peppers in half, remove seeds and dip shells into boiling water for 1 minute. Combine and mix thoroughly the meat, rice, garlic, onion, egg and seasonings. Heap the mixture into the green pepper shells and place in a greased baking dish.

In a saucepan bring to a boil the tomato sauce, water, fructose and vinegar. Spoon over the stuffed peppers. Bake at 350 degrees 45 minutes to 1 hour.

4 servings

Cabbage Stuffed with Ground Beef

12 large cabbage leaves
1 lb. ground lean beef
1 clove garlic, minced
¼ cup minced onions
3 tbsps. chopped parsley
1 tsp. salt
½ tsp. thyme
¼ tsp. white pepper
1 egg
2 tbsps. fructose
3 tbsps. vinegar
1 can tomato sauce, 7½-oz.
¼ cup hot water

Place cabbage leaves in boiling water just long enough to soften. Drain. Mix the rest of the ingredients thoroughly. Divide in 12 portions. Wrap a cabbage leaf around each one and fasten with a toothpick. Place in buttered casserole and pour tomato sauce and water over the stuffed cabbage rolls. Cover and bake for one hour or until tender at 350 degrees. Uncover for the last 15 minutes.

4 servings

Aloha Sweetbreads

1 lb. sweetbreads
1 tbsp. vinegar
water
1 onion
1 green pepper
1 cup crushed pineapple with juice
2 tbsps. lemon juice
2 tbsps. fructose
2 tbsps. peanut oil
1 tsp. ginger
½ tsp. salt

Place sweetbreads and vinegar in a saucepan. Add water to cover the sweetbreads and bring to a boil. Simmer for 15 minutes. Let cool and remove membrane and gristle. Break into chunks. Cut the onion into wedges (about 1 cup) and place in a skillet with the sweetbread chunks and peanut oil. Cook over low heat until onions are golden. Add the remaining ingredients, cover and simmer over low heat for 15 minutes. This may be served over rice or noodles.

3-4 servings

Sweet and Sour Pork

1 lb. pork shoulder cut in ½-inch
cubes
1 tbsp. soy sauce
2 tbsps. flour
peanut or other oil for deep frying
1 cup green pepper cut in 1-inch
squares
2 cloves garlic, mashed
2 carrots sliced in Julienne strips
½ cup sliced onion
1 cup canned pineapple chunks
preserved in natural unsweetened
juice
1½ cups water
3 tbsps. vinegar
1 tbsp. fructose
1 tbsp. cornstarch

Moisten the pork in soy sauce and shake in a small bag with the flour. Fry in deep fat at 375 degrees until golden brown, about 10 minutes. Place in heavy frying pan with green pepper, garlic, carrot strips, onion, pineapple chunks and 1 cup of water. Cover and cook for 10 minutes. Mix the vinegar, fructose and cornstarch in ½ cup water. Stir into frying pan mixture and cook until slightly thickened, about five minutes.

Serve with steamed rice.

4 servings

Hawaiian Lamb Patties

1 lb. ground lamb
¼ cup minced onions
¼ cup cornstarch
2 tsps. soy sauce
¼ tsp. salt
⅓ cup chopped mushrooms
1 tbsp. vegetable oil
1 cup unsweetened pineapple juice
2 tbsps. fructose
4 tbsps. lemon juice
1 tbsp. soy sauce

Mix thoroughly the lamb, onion, corn-starch, soy sauce and salt. Divide this mixture into 16 parts and flatten each part. Place a rounded teaspoon of the chopped mushroom in center of each part and shape into 16 patties with mushroom centers. Brown in oil over medium heat.

Combine the pineapple juice, fructose, lemon juice, and soy sauce in a casserole or glass deep pie dish. Place the patties in this dish and turn so that they are coated on all sides. Bake at 400 degrees for 30 minutes turning the patties at least twice during this time.

This is also very good using other juices such as orange, cranberry, blueberry, etc., instead of the pineapple juice. The cooked liquid may be thickened with cornstarch or flour and served with the patties over rice or noodles.

16 patties

The Fructose Cookbook

Eggs in a Golden Nest

1 recipe Zesty Carrots
4 eggs
½ cup grated cheese

Prepare carrots according to recipe. After cooking for 7 minutes, make 4 wells in the vegetables using the bottom of a cup or glass. Break each egg carefully into a saucer and slide it into a well. Sprinkle with grated cheese—cheddar, parmesan or Swiss. Cover and cook over low heat until eggs are set up to your liking.

4 servings

Greek Casserole

1 tbsp. fructose
1 egg
¼ lb. feta cheese
½ cup minced onion
1 medium eggplant
2 tomatoes
½ tsp. oregano
½ tsp. basil
½ tsp. coriander
salt and pepper to taste

Beat egg and fructose. Add cheese and mix thoroughly. Slice tomatoes and eggplant into ¼-inch slices. Sprinkle a layer of onions on the bottom of a buttered casserole. Over this place a layer of eggplant. Spread feta cheese mixture over the eggplant and top with tomato slices sprinkled with herbs. Continue with the layers until you have used up all of the ingredients ending with tomatoes and herbs. Bake at 375 degrees for 30 minutes or until casserole is bubbly.

4 servings

Feta Cheese Pancakes

2 eggs, separated
2 tbsps. fructose
½ lb. feta cheese
¼ cup ground sunflower seeds
¼ cup bran
salt to taste
oil for frying

Beat together the egg yolks and fructose until light. Combine thoroughly with the cheese, ground sunflower seeds and bran. My experience has been that the salt content of feta cheese varies, so add salt carefully. Beat the egg whites stiff, but not dry, and fold into the mixture. Drop by rounded tablespoons into hot oil and spread lightly with the back of a spoon. Brown on both sides and serve hot with fruit sauces.

8 pancakes

Brownie Blintzes

Batter:
½ cup flour
¼ cup powdered carob
1 tbsp. fructose
½ tsp. salt
2 eggs plus 1 egg white
½ cup water

Filling:

1 cup dry cheese,
ricotta or baker's
2 tbsps. fructose
½ tsp. cinnamon
¼ tsp. salt
1 egg yolk
2 tsps. melted butter
or margarine

Combine thoroughly the flour, carob, fructose and salt. (I use a large glass measuring pitcher for this.) Beat in the eggs and water to make a thin batter.

In a small bowl mix thoroughly all these ingredients. I use my favorite six-inch frying pan for melting the butter so that it is ready for preparing the crepes.

Pour about 2 tbsps. of the batter onto a hot, lightly buttered 6-inch frying pan, turning the pan from side to side so that the batter spreads evenly. Fry on one side only, just until the visible side is set. Turn onto a wooden board, cooked side up. Place a scant tbsp. of the filling in the center of each crepe. Fold the sides over the filling and tuck the edges over to make an envelope. The timing works out well if you fill each crepe while the next one is frying. You will occasionally need to add a small amount of butter to the frying pan. Also towards the end you may want to add a small amount of water to the batter. When ready to serve, fry until lightly browned on both sides. These can be served with sour cream.

A versatile dish, blintzes also make a delicious brunch or dessert topped with berries or sliced fruit.

12-14 blintzes

Ceviche

1 lb. fish fillets, cubed (halibut,
tuna, mauhi-mauhi, sole, etc.)
2 cups diced tomatoes
½ cup lime juice
1 tsp. fructose
2 tbsps. finely chopped onion
2 tsps. salt
¼ tsp. oregano
1 tsp. white pepper
3 dashes tabasco sauce

Layer the fish and the tomatoes, approximately four layers, in a quart jar, distributing
the seasonings evenly. Cover with lime juice.
Let stand in refrigerator for 24 hours.

4 servings

Fish Baked in Marinating Sauce

2 lbs. fish fillets
2 tbsps. soy sauce
1 tbsp. fructose
2 tbsps. lemon juice
1 tbsp. Dijon type mustard
1 tsp. finely chopped garlic
½ tsp. ground ginger

Place the fish fillets in a buttered shallow baking dish in one layer. Combine the remaining ingredients and spread over the fish. Let it marinate about 45 minutes. Bake covered at 350 degrees 25 to 35 minutes until done. Timing depends on the thickness of the fish.

4 servings

Oriental Shrimp with Vegetables

1 clove garlic
½ cup sliced celery
½ cup sliced onion
½ cup sliced green pepper
½ cup sliced mushrooms
2 tbsps. oil
⅓ cup vinegar
2 tbsps. fructose
2 tsps. soy sauce
1 cup tomato juice
1 tbsp. corn starch
¼ cup cold water
2 cans shrimp (4½-oz. each) or
½-lb. fresh shrimp
½ cup sliced cooked carrots
¼ cup slivered almonds (optional)

Sauté the garlic, celery, onion, green pepper and mushrooms in the oil just until tender. Combine vinegar, fructose, soy sauce and tomato juice. Pour into sautéed vegetables and bring to a boil. Dissolve corn starch in water and gradually add to simmering sauce, stirring constantly until thickened. Add shrimp and carrots and bring to a boil once more. Remove from heat. This is very good served with rice. A topping of slivered almonds adds a delicious finishing touch.

4 servings

Main Courses

79

Sauces and Syrups

Applesauce

4 cups diced cooking apples
½ cup water
¼ cup fructose

The amounts of water and fructose may vary according to the juiciness and sweetness of the apples. Cook apples and water in a saucepan until apples are tender. Add fructose and simmer one minute. If you prefer a purée, force this through a coarse sieve.

6 servings

Lemony Applesauce

Add 2 tbsps. lemon juice to the above recipe, or 1 tbsp. juice and 1 tbsp. grated lemon rind. Correct the amount of fructose to taste.

6 servings

Sauces and Syrups

81

Spice Applesauce

Add 1 tsp. of any of the following spices combined to your taste: cinnamon, ginger, cloves, nutmeg, allspice.

6 servings

Apple-Mint Sauce

Add ⅓ cup chopped fresh mint or ¼ cup dried mint 2 minutes before adding fructose.

6 servings

Applesauce also combines well with other fruits such as blueberries, pineapple and plums.

Fructose Cranberry Sauce

1 lb. cranberries
1 cup water
1 cup fructose

Place cranberries and water in a saucepan. Cover and bring to a boil. Simmer until cranberries begin to pop. Add the fructose and continue cooking until all of the cranberries have popped.

Spiced Cranberry Sauce

Add to the above recipe about 2 tsps. of spices to your taste. For example, ¼ tsp. nutmeg, ¾ tsp. cinnamon, ½ tsp. ground cloves, ½ tsp. ground allspice.

8-10 servings

Minted Cranberry Sauce

1 cup mint tea
1 package (1 lb.) cranberries
1 cup fructose

Make a strong mint tea, steeping 1 tbsp. of crushed mint leaves in 1 cup of water for at least fifteen minutes. Cook the tea and cranberries together until the berries begin to pop. Add the fructose and cook on low heat another ten minutes.

8-10 servings

Strawberry-Cranberry Sauce

4 cups cranberries
1 cup water
2 cups sliced strawberries
1 cup fructose
½ tsp. almond extract (optional)

Cook cranberries in a covered saucepan until they pop. Add strawberries and fructose. Bring to a boil and simmer for 5 minutes. If desired, add almond flavoring.

This is good to use in place of cranberry sauce with meats. It also can be used as a sauce with puddings or to replace syrup with pancakes and waffles.

10-12 servings

Rhubarb Sauce

4 cups rhubarb, washed, sliced
and cut in 1-inch pieces
½ cup water
½ cup fructose, more or less
1 tsp. cinnamon
½ tsp. nutmeg

Bring the rhubarb and water to a boil. Simmer until it is tender, 10 to 15 minutes. Add water as necessary to prevent scorching. Add the fructose and spices and reheat. The amount of fructose may vary depending on the tartness of the rhubarb and the individual taste.

8 servings

Maple-flavored Syrup

1 cup fructose
⅓ cup water
¼ tsp. maple flavoring

In a small saucepan combine the fructose and water. Bring to a boil and simmer for three minutes. Add the maple flavoring.

When used on pancakes or waffles, this syrup is very good when heated with a tablespoon of margarine or butter.

⅔ cup

Mocha Syrup

²⁄₃ cup fructose
1 cup carob powder
2 tsps. decaffeinated coffee
1 cup water

In a saucepan mix together the fructose, carob powder and decaffeinated coffee. Stir in the water and bring to a boil, stirring constantly. Cook on low heat for two minutes while continuing to stir.

This sauce is delicious on babas as well as puddings and sherbets.

1 ¼ cups

Rum Syrup

½ cup water
½ cup fructose
¼ cup rum

Bring to a boil the fructose and water. Let simmer 3 to 10 minutes depending on the use to which you will put the syrup. Rum syrup is traditional with babas or savarins. When so used, the syrup should be quite thin so that it will better permeate the cakes.

²⁄₃ cup

Desserts and Confections

Tropical Carrot Cake

2 tsps. baking soda
1 tsp. salt
2 tsps. cinnamon
2 cups flour
1 cup vegetable oil
1¼ cups fructose
4 eggs
1 tsp. vanilla
2 cups grated carrots
1 cup raisins
1 cup chopped nuts
1 cup shredded coconut

Sift together the first four ingredients.
Cream together the oil and fructose. Beat in the eggs one at a time. Add vanilla. Beat in the mixture of salt, baking soda, cinnamon and flour. Stir in the carrots, raisins, coconuts and nuts. Bake in a greased 13 x 9 x 2-inch pan at 350 degrees for 40 to 50 minutes until lightly browned, or until an inserted toothpick comes out clean.

12 servings

Banana-Prune Cake

¼ cup margarine or butter
½ cup fructose
1 egg
2 tbsps. buttermilk
½ tsp. vanilla
1 cup white flour
¼ tsp. salt
½ tsp. soda
½ cup mashed bananas
¼ cup chopped prunes

Cream together the fructose and the margarine. Beat in the egg. Sift together the flour, salt and soda and add with the buttermilk and vanilla, beating thoroughly. Beat in the bananas and prunes until well mixed. Turn into a greased and floured 8-inch cake tin. Bake at 325 degrees for one hour.

This can be served with slightly sweetened whipped cream or ice cream. It is also very good just plain.

The recipe can be varied by substituting other fruits for the prunes, such as raisins, chopped dates, chopped dried apricots. One-fourth cup chopped nuts may also be added.

6-8 servings

Rhubarb Teaparty Cake

Streusel topping:
¼ cup margarine
6 tbsps. fructose
6 tbsps. flour
1 tsp. cinnamon

Cake batter:
½ cup margarine or butter
1 cup fructose
2 eggs
2½ cups sifted flour
1 tsp. baking powder
1 tsp. soda
½ tsp. salt
1 cup buttermilk
2 cups finely sliced rhubarb

Mix these ingredients together until crumbly and set aside.

Cream thoroughly the margarine with the fructose. Beat in the eggs thoroughly one at a time. Sift together the dry ingredients and add alternately with the buttermilk, beating thoroughly. Stir in the rhubarb. Spread the batter in a greased 13 x 9-inch pan and sprinkle the streusel evenly over the batter. Bake in a 350-degree oven until toothpick inserted comes out clean, about 40 to 45 minutes. The rhubarb tends to settle to the lower part of the cake, giving it an interesting variety of textures from the moist bottom to the crisp streusel topping. This can be served happily with either whipped cream or ice cream.

12 servings

Whole Wheat Apple Cake

1 cup whole wheat flour
⅓ cup fructose
1 tsp. cinnamon
¼ tsp. salt
3 tbsps. margarine or butter
½ tsp. soda
¾ cup chopped apple
1 egg
½ cup buttermilk

Mix together the flour, fructose, cinnamon and salt. Cut the margarine into this mixture until it is crumbly. Reserve 6 tbsps. of this mixture for the topping. To the remainder add ½ tsp. soda and ¾ cup chopped apple. (I use pippins for this.) Beat together the egg and buttermilk. Combine thoroughly with the crumb and apple mixture. Spread in a 9-inch round dish. Sprinkle with reserved crumb mixture. Bake at 375 degrees for thirty minutes or until toothpick comes out clean.

8 servings

French Baba, modified

½ cup scalded milk
4 tbsps. butter or margarine
3 tbsps. warm water
1 tbsp. dry yeast
3 tbsps. fructose
2 eggs
2 tbsps. grated orange
  or lemon rind (optional)
2 cups flour (approximately)
¼ tsp. salt

Melt butter in scalded milk. Cool to lukewarm. Dissolve yeast and 1 tbsp. fructose in the warm water. Add to butter and milk with remaining fructose. Beat in the eggs and stir in the rest of the ingredients to make a soft, slightly sticky dough. The amount of flour will depend on the size of the eggs. Turn onto well-floured board and knead until dough is smooth, at least five minutes. Place in a greased bowl, cover with a damp towel and put in a warm place until it has doubled.

For traditional babas break off enough dough to fill ⅓ of greased muffin tins; or if you wish, this entire dough can be baked as a cake in a bundt pan or casserole. Oil the tops. Allow to rise until muffin tins are filled or cake has doubled. Bake small babas in 375-degree oven about 15 minutes until lightly browned. Bake cake in 350-degree oven 40 to 50 minutes until lightly browned. While still warm, prick all over with a fork, place in a dish that can catch the drippings and pour over the babas or cake any warm syrup you prefer.

These keep very well in a freezer and can be heated in a 300-degree oven for 15 minutes before using. For a kind of continental breakfast I enjoy the muffins heated simply with margarine and jam.

12 small babas

Carob-Mocha Cake

2 tsps. instant decaf. coffee
1 cup boiling water
1 ¼ cups fructose
¾ cup carob powder
1 ¼ cups all-purpose flour
1 tsp. salt
2 tsps. baking soda
1 tsp. baking powder
1 cup buttermilk
2 eggs
1 tsp. vanilla
½ cup vegetable oil

Dissolve instant decaffeinated coffee in boiling water. Let cool to lukewarm. Meanwhile combine dry ingredients in mixing bowl, stirring thoroughly. Add eggs, buttermilk, oil, vanilla and water containing the dissolved coffee. Beat until well-mixed, about 5 minutes by hand or 2 minutes at medium speed if using electric mixer. This will make a thin batter. Bake in a 13 x 9 x 2-inch oblong pan or two 9-inch layer cake pans. Oven temperature should be 350 degrees. Baking time for oblong pan is about 35 minutes; for layers, about 30 minutes.

12 servings

Mock Chocolate Upside Down Cupcakes

¼ cup melted margarine or butter
¼ cup fructose
½ cup crushed pineapple (or other diced fruit)
½ cup hot water
1 tsp. instant coffee
½ cup fructose
½ cup ground carob
¾ cup flour
½ tsp. salt
1 tsp. baking soda
½ tsp. maple flavoring
1 egg
½ cup buttermilk

Place 1 tsp. of melted margarine in each of 12 muffin tins. Stir well 1 tsp. of fructose into each of these. Allow to cool. Spread heaping tsp. of crushed pineapple over each of these.

Dissolve the coffee in the hot water and allow to cool. Stir together in a mixing bowl the fructose, carob flour, salt and baking soda. Beat the egg into the buttermilk. Add the coffee and maple flavoring. Pour the liquid ingredients into the dry ingredients about ¼ at a time, mixing thoroughly after each addition. Spread the batter in each muffin tin so that it is a little more than half full. Bake at 350 degrees about 30 minutes until a toothpick inserted comes out clean. Let stand for about 10 minutes. It may be necessary to run a spatula around the sides to loosen. Invert the muffin tins over a sheet of aluminum foil.

12 cupcakes

My Favorite Cheese Cake

Crust:
¼ cup melted margarine or butter
1 cup ground sunflower seeds
½ cup ground almonds
2 tsps. cinnamon
2 tbsps. fructose

Filling:
1 cup baker's cheese (or ricotta)
½ cup fructose
4 eggs, separated
¼ cup water
2 tbsps. lime juice
1 tbsp. lime rind chopped fine
¼ tsp. salt

Combine crust ingredients and press firmly to line baking dish. Beat egg whites to soft peaks. Blend yolks and fructose. Mix in liquid ingredients and lime rind. Then beat in the baker's cheese and salt. Fold in the beaten egg whites. Pour into lined baking dish. Bake at 325 degrees for 1 hour. Let cool in oven.

I like to use ground seeds. Your favorite general cook book can supply you with more conventional crusts such as zweiback, or you might want to try lining your baking dish with soaked and drained rye crackers or matzos.

Something else I like to do is to dribble a bit of marmalade or plum jam over the top just after turning off the oven, then letting it set while cheese cake cools.

8 servings

Tapioca-Cheese Pudding

2 tbsps. margarine or butter
2 tbsps. fructose
1 tsp. cinnamon
1¼ cups cornflake crumbs
2 tbsps. quick-cooking tapioca
¼ tsp. salt
1 tbsp. fructose
½ tsp. cinnamon
1 cup milk
1½ cups pot cheese (or ricotta)
3 eggs, separated
¼ tsp. salt
2 tbsps. lemon juice
1 tsp. grated lemon rind
½ cup fructose
⅓ cup sliced dates
2 tbsps. slivered almonds

Melt margarine. Mix with 2 tbsps. fructose, 1 tsp. cinnamon and the cornflake crumbs. Reserve ¼ cup of this mixture. Spread the rest firmly on the bottom of a glass baking dish.

In a saucepan place the tapioca mixed with ¼ tsp. salt, one tbsp. fructose and ½ tsp. cinnamon. Gradually add the milk and cook, stirring constantly, until it comes to a boil. Let cool 15 minutes. Stir and chill.

Mix until smooth the pot cheese, egg yolks, ¼ tsp. salt, grated lemon rind and juice, and ½ cup fructose. Blend this mixture in with the chilled tapioca mixture. Fold in the dates and almonds. Beat egg whites until stiff but not dry. Fold into the combined mixtures. Pour into the cornflake-crust lined baking dish. Sprinkle with the reserved cornflake mixture. Bake at 300 degrees for 1-1½ hours, or until toothpick comes out clean. Turn off heat and let cool in the oven with door partly open.

10 servings

No-Bake Orange-Cheese Dessert

1 envelope unflavored gelatin
⅓ cup fructose
1/8 tsp. salt
2 tbsps. water
½ cup milk
1 egg, separated
2 tbsps. grated orange peel
1 orange, peeled and cut into small chunks
1 tsp. vanilla
1 cup cereal crumbs, such as rice krispies or corn flakes
1 tbsp. fructose
½ tsp. nutmeg
2 tbsps. melted butter or margarine
1½ cups ricotta cheese

Mix thoroughly gelatin, 1 tbsp. of fructose, salt and water in top of double boiler. Add milk, egg yolk and remainder of fructose. Mix thoroughly and cook over boiling water, stirring until the gelatin is dissolved, about 5 minutes. Remove from heat, add grated orange peel and chunks and vanilla. Stir well and chill. Meanwhile, prepare topping by combining crumbs, 1 tbs. fructose and nutmeg. Mix thoroughly with melted butter. When gelatin mixture is thick but not firm, remove from refrigerator and combine with ricotta cheese. Beat egg white until stiff but not dry. Fold into mixture. Turn into a glass or pottery dish and sprinkle with topping. Chill until firm.

8 servings

Yam Chiffon Pie

1 envelope gelatin
⅓ plus ¼ cup fructose
½ tsp. salt
1 tsp. cinnamon
½ tsp. nutmeg
½ cup milk
3 eggs, separated
1½ cups cooked, mashed yams
1 9-inch baked pie shell

Combine thoroughly in a saucepan the gelatin, ⅓ cup fructose, salt, cinnamon and nutmeg. Stir in the milk, egg yolks and yams and mix well. Cook, stirring constantly until gelatin is dissolved and contents heated, about 10 minutes. Chill in refrigerator until slightly thickened. Beat egg whites until stiff but not dry and stir in ¼ cup fructose. Fold the gelatin mixture into the sweetened egg whites. Pour into baked pie shell and chill.

For variety I like to use the shell with corn-flakes and coconut described in the recipe for Triple Treat Lemon Chiffon Pie.

6-8 servings

Pumpkin Chiffon Pie

In the above recipe substitute 1½ cups canned or cooked pumpkin for the yams and use ½ cup fructose instead of ⅓ in the gelatin mixture.

6-8 servings

Triple Treat Lemon Chiffon Pie

¼ cup margarine or butter
2 tbsps. fructose
1 cup crushed cornflakes
1 cup flaked coconut
⅓ cup ground sunflower seeds
2 tbsps. ground sesame seeds

1 ½ cups blueberries
¼ cup fructose
¼ tsp. almond flavoring
1 tsp. cornstarch

1 envelope gelatin
⅔ cup fructose, divided
1/8 tsp. salt
¼ cup water
½ cup lemon juice
4 eggs, separated
2 tsps. grated lemon rind

Melt the margarine in the bottom of a pie dish 9 inches in diameter and 2 inches deep. Combine 2 tbsps. fructose, cornflakes, coconut, ground sunflower seeds and sesame seeds. Mix thoroughly with the margarine and press down in the bottom and sides of the pie dish. Bake until lightly browned at 400 degrees, about 15 minutes.

Place the blueberries, ¼ cup fructose, almond flavoring and cornstarch in a small saucepan and simmer until thick. The water clinging to the blueberries after you rinse them should be sufficient. Spread blueberry layer over baked crust.

In top of a double boiler mix gelatin, ⅓ cup fructose and salt. Separate the eggs. Stir the water, lemon juice and egg yolks into the dry mixture and cook, stirring constantly until the gelatin is dissolved. Beat egg whites until stiff. Stir in the grated lemon rind and the remaining ⅓ cup fructose. Fold the gelatin mixture into the egg white mixture. Pour into the pie dish over the blueberry layer. Place in refrigerator until firm.

Tart cherries or other berries may be substituted for the blueberries.

8 servings

Carob Brownies

½ cup fructose
½ cup carob powder
½ cup melted margarine or butter
3 eggs
2 tsps. vanilla
½ cup whole wheat flour
½ cup white flour
¼ tsp. salt
1 tsp. baking powder
½ cup chopped nuts

Mix thoroughly the fructose and carob powder. Combine with the melted margarine and cream well. Add vanilla and beat in the eggs one at a time. Sift together the flours, salt and baking powder. Add to the first mixture and beat thoroughly. Add nuts and mix well. Spread in a greased 10-inch square pan. Bake at 350 degrees about 25 minutes. Cool and cut in squares.

25 brownies

Ginger-Carob Thins

½ cup margarine or butter
1 cup fructose
½ cup carob powder
2 eggs
1 cup flour
¼ tsp. salt
1 tsp. baking powder
2 tsps. ginger

In a mixing bowl cream the margarine. Combine the fructose and carob powder. Add to the margarine and cream well. Beat in the eggs one at a time. Sift together the flour, salt, baking powder and ginger. Add to the first mixture and beat thoroughly. Spread in a greased cookie tin 10 x 15 x 1-inch deep. Bake at 350 degrees 20 to 25 minutes. Cut into squares or diamonds.

50 cookies

Zucchini Bars

½ cup butter or margarine
⅔ cup fructose
2 cups flour
2 tsps. baking powder
⅔ cup shredded coconut
2 eggs
½ tsp. salt
2 cups shredded zucchini
⅔ cup dates, sliced
1 tsp. vanilla

Cream butter and fructose. Beat in eggs and vanilla until blended. Mix together flour, salt and baking powder. Add gradually to creamed mixture and beat until blended. Stir in the zucchini, dates and coconuts. Spread the mixture in a greased 10 x 15-inch pan and bake at 350 degrees for 40 minutes or until nicely browned on top and inserted toothpick comes out clean. Cut into bars, after cooling on rack.

25 bars

Beverley's Lemon Thins, adapted

Shortbread Layer:
½ cup margarine or butter
¼ cup fructose
1 cup all-purpose flour
¼ tsp. salt

Lemon Topping:
2 eggs
⅔ cup fructose
2 tbsps. flour
3 or 4 tbsps. lemon juice*

Ingredients should be at room temperature. Mix and cut together until crumbly. Press into a 9 x 9-inch pan. Bake at 350 degrees until just beginning to brown, about 20 minutes.

Beat eggs lightly. Combine fructose and flour. Add with lemon juice to eggs and beat until thoroughly mixed. Pour over shortbread and bake at 350 degrees until top is just dry but not brown, about 20 minutes. Wait until cool, then cut into squares.

*Beverley says to use 3 tbsps. lemon juice. I personally like it just a bit more tart.

3 dozen 1½-inch squares

Rice Krispie Peanut Butter Bars

1 cup fructose
½ cup water
1 cup peanut butter
4 cups rice krispies

Stirring until fructose is dissolved, cook fructose and water until it reaches the soft ball stage when tested in cold water. Remove from heat and stir in peanut butter immediately. Combine with rice krispies and spread in a 13 x 9 x 2-inch pan. Allow to stand until cool. Cut into bars.

It is important to work quickly once the fructose syrup is ready. If you wish, you may spread a layer of melted chocolate chips over the pan of cookies while still warm. Other cereals may also be used.

2 dozen bars

Mrs. Ginsburg's Cookies, modified

½ cup margarine or butter
⅓ cup fructose
½ cup ricotta cheese
2 eggs
⅔ cup rice flour
1½ cups unbleached white flour
1 tsp. baking powder
½ tsp. soda
2 tbsps. sesame seeds
Your favorite jam or jelly

Cream together the margarine, fructose and ricotta cheese. Beat in the eggs. Sift together the flours, baking powder and soda. Combine with the sesame seeds and stir into the first mixture. Blend to make a soft dough. Refrigerate until firm. Divide into 6 balls. On a well-floured board roll each one out thin to form an oblong about 4 by 8 inches. Spread the oblongs with jam or jelly and roll up jelly roll fashion moistening the edge to hold together. Bake these rolls at 300 degrees for 45 minutes. After they cool, slice in ¼ inch slices with a sharp knife to form pinwheel cookies.

7 dozen cookies

Desserts and Confections

Almond Crisps

½ cup fructose
½ cup butter or margarine
2 cups ground almonds

Heat margarine at low temperature just until melted. Mix almonds and fructose and add to shortening, blending well. Spread out on lightly floured board or waxed paper and shape into an oblong about 1/8-inch thick. Cut into diamond shapes and, lifting with a spatula, place on ungreased cookie sheet about ½-inch apart. Bake at 325 degrees until lightly browned, about 20 minutes. Allow to cool slightly before removing from pan.

40 cookies

Sesame Cookies

2 ¼ cups flour
¼ tsp. salt
⅓ cup toasted sesame seeds
¾ cup margarine or butter
¾ cup fructose
1 egg
1 tsp. vanilla

Sift together the flour and salt, stir in the sesame seeds. In a mixing bowl cream together the margarine and fructose. Add the egg, beating until light. Stir in the vanilla. Add the sifted flour, salt and sesame seed mixture in three stages beating thoroughly after each addition. Form into balls about ¾" diameter. Place on an ungreased cookie sheet, flattening each ball slightly. Bake at 350 degrees for 20 minutes.

4 dozen cookies

Cinnamon Nuggets

½ cup whole wheat flour
1 cup unbleached white flour
1 tsp. cream of tartar
½ tsp. baking soda
¼ tsp. salt
½ cup margarine or butter
⅔ cup fructose
1 egg
½ tsp. almond extract
4 tsps. fructose
1 ½ tsps. cinnamon

Sift together the two kinds of flour, cream of tartar, soda and salt. Cream together the margarine and ⅔ cup fructose. Beat in the egg and almond extract. Stir in the sifted dry ingredients and mix thoroughly. Place in refrigerator until firm enough to handle. Meanwhile, combine the 4 tsps. fructose and cinnamon in a small bowl or glass. Shape the dough into balls the size of a small walnut. Roll the balls one at a time in the fructose and cinnamon mixture. Place on a greased baking sheet. Bake at 350 degrees approximately 20 minutes.

3 dozen cookies

Carob Oatmeal Cookies

½ cup oatmeal
¾ cup white flour
3 tbsps. carob powder
¼ tsp. baking soda
1 tsp. cinnamon
¼ cup margarine or butter
½ cup fructose
1 egg
¼ cup buttermilk
1 tsp. vanilla

Combine the oatmeal, flour, carob powder, soda and cinnamon in a small bowl. In a mixing bowl cream the margarine together with the fructose. Stir in the egg and buttermilk until well-blended. Add the vanilla. Add the dry ingredients in 4 parts, beating well after each addition. Drop by teaspoons on a well-greased cookie tin, allowing room for spreading. Bake until no longer glossy at 350 degrees, about 20 minutes.

30 cookies

Oatmeal Raisin Cookies

¾ cup white flour
¼ tsp. baking soda
½ tsp. cinnamon
½ tsp. ginger
½ cup oatmeal
¼ cup margarine or butter
½ cup fructose
1 egg
¼ cup buttermilk
1 cup raisins

Stir together the flour, baking soda, cinnamon, ginger and oatmeal. In another mixing bowl, cream together the margarine and fructose. Beat in the egg until smooth. Add the buttermilk and the mixture of dry ingredients. Beat until thoroughly mixed. Stir in the raisins. Drop from a teaspoon onto a greased cookie sheet 1½ inches apart. Bake at 350 degrees until nicely browned, about 20 minutes.

50 cookies

Lacy Popcorn Cookies

2 tbsps. butter or margarine
⅔ cup fructose
2 eggs, beaten
1 tsp. strawberry extract (or other flavoring)
½ tsp. baking powder
2½ cups chopped popcorn
¼ cup flour

Cream the butter and fructose. Add the beaten eggs and flavoring. Stir thoroughly. Beat in the flour, baking powder and popcorn. Drop by teaspoonsful onto a greased pan about one inch apart. Spread them with a spatula. Bake at 300 degrees for 20 minutes. Remove at once with spatula. If these cookies should lose their crispness after a day or two, they can be restored by heating at 300 degrees for 5 minutes.

3 dozen

Elizabeth's Filled Cookies

Filling:
1 cup ground raisins or dates
⅓ cup fructose
1 tbsp. flour
½ cup water

Cookie dough:
⅔ cup fructose
½ cup margarine
1 egg
3½ to 4 cups flour
1 tsp. baking soda
2 tsps. cream of tartar
1 tsp. nutmeg
1 tsp. vanilla
½ cup milk

Stirring constantly, heat the filling ingredients together in a saucepan until thick. Allow to cool before using.

Cream together the margarine and fructose. Beat in the egg. Sift together the dry ingredients and add alternately with the milk, mixing well to form a soft dough. Chill for easier handling. Roll very thin on a well-floured board. Cut in 2½-inch circles. For each cookie place ½ tsp. of filling in center of one circle, cover it with another circle and press the edges together. Place the filled cookies on a greased cookie sheet and bake at 400 degrees about 10 minutes. If there is any dough left over, it can be cut into shapes and sprinkled with fructose and cinnamon, one tsp. of cinnamon to 2 tbsps. fructose.

40 cookies

Fruited Marvel Pudding

3 tbsps. cornstarch
1 cup fructose, divided
1 tbsp. lime juice
2 cups sliced strawberries
⅓ cup melted margarine or butter
2 cups rice krispies
1½ cups buttermilk
1 tsp. vanilla
1 egg, beaten
1½ cups flour
1½ tsp. baking soda
½ tsp. salt

Mix thoroughly the cornstarch and ½ cup fructose in a saucepan. Stir in the lime juice and strawberries. Cook over low heat, stirring constantly until mixture thickens. Mix the margarine and rice krispies in a mixing bowl. Stir in the buttermilk, vanilla and beaten egg. Sift together the flour, remaining half cup of fructose, baking soda and salt. Stir these dry ingredients into the mixture in the mixing bowl just enough to moisten. Turn into a 12 x 8-inch oblong pan. Spread the strawberry mixture over the top of the batter and cut through as you would for a marble cake. Bake in a 375-degree oven 40 to 45 minutes until golden brown and a toothpick comes out clean.

This is very good served with whipped cream or ice cream. Other fruits, such as blueberries or raspberries, may be substituted for the strawberries.

16 servings

Frozen Fruit Custard

⅓ cup fructose
1 tbsp. cornstarch
1½ cups hot milk
2 egg yolks
2 egg whites
1 tsp. vanilla
1 cup whipping cream
1 cup chopped nuts
1 cup sliced fruit

Combine the fructose and cornstarch in the top of a double boiler. Stir in the hot milk and cook over lightly boiling water for 15 minutes, stirring from time to time. Beat the egg yolks in a large bowl. Gradually stir in the liquid mixture. Cool in refrigerator. Beat egg whites until stiff. Fold into chilled mixture. Whip the cream and fold in with the vanilla. Fold in the chopped nuts and the fruit. Pour into a refrigerator tray and freeze.

1 cup chilled and whipped evaporated milk may be substituted for the whipping cream. Also ½ cup powdered skim milk and ½ cup ice water can be whipped, adding 2 tbsps. lemon juice towards the end of the whipping.
6 servings

Banana-Pineapple Sherbet

½ cup fructose
1 envelope gelatin
½ cup water
1 cup pineapple juice
1 cup crushed unsweetened pineapple
2 cups buttermilk
1½ cups mashed bananas

Combine the fructose and gelatin in a saucepan. Add water and stir constantly over low heat until the gelatin is dissolved. Stir the remaining ingredients into the gelatin mixture. Pour into freezing trays and set in freezer until the mixture is thick but not solid. Remove to a bowl and beat until smooth. Return to freezing trays and freeze until firm.

This recipe works well with other fruits and fruit combinations such as peaches, strawberries, papaya, etc. Sliced almonds or other chopped nuts are also a good addition.

6 servings

Gelatin Candies

4 envelopes gelatin
2 cups fructose
1/8 tsp. salt
2½ cups water
2 tbsps. lemon juice
2 tbsps. grated lemon rind (optional)
1 cup ground nuts
or sunflower seeds or
grated coconut

This recipe is inspired by the jellied candies served in Balkan countries with small cups of syrupy coffee. Traditionally they are rolled in powdered sugar, but since users of this book are avoiding such sugars, I am suggesting more wholesome alternatives.

Combine gelatin, fructose and salt in a saucepan. Mix in the water and bring to a boil, stirring constantly. Let simmer for 15 minutes. Remove from heat and stir in the lemon juice and the rind, if used. Pour into an 8 x 8-inch pan. Let stand for 6 hours or more. Do not refrigerate. Cut into oblongs 2 x 1 inches. Roll in the ground nuts, sunflower seeds or coconut.

This recipe adapts itself to many delicious variations. You may stir in a cup of grated carrots or a cup of chopped dried apricots. A cup of drained crushed pineapple can be us-ed and with this you may substitute a half cup of the pineapple juice for a half cup of the water. Two teaspoons of instant decaf-feinated coffee may be added, in which case you would omit the lemon juice and rind. Chopped nuts or sesame seeds may be used in any of these variations.

64 1-inch squares

Carob and Cheese Balls

¼ cup fructose
1 cup ricotta cheese
½ tsp. maple flavoring
½ cup ground sesame seeds
¼ cup carob powder
1/8 tsp. salt
⅓ cup shredded coconut

Mix thoroughly the ingredients, except the coconut, in the order given. Chill about 15 minutes for easier handling. Form into balls, using about a teaspoon of the mixture. Pressing lightly, roll each ball in the coconut. Store in refrigerator.

This delicious confection is a great boon to sufferers with acne or anyone else having problems with chocolate.

about 3 dozen

Pickles and Preserves

Pickled Herring

1 ¼ cups vinegar
½ cup water
⅓ cup fructose
2 cups herring pieces
¾ cup sliced purple onion
¾ cup sliced carrots (optional)
1 tsp. whole cloves
2 tsps. mustard seed
2 tbsps. horseradish
3 bay leaves

The herring should be cleaned and soaked in salt water overnight. Rinse thoroughly and cut into one-inch pieces. Bring vinegar, water and fructose to a boil, stirring until the fructose is dissolved. Allow to cool. Place in layers in a one-quart jar starting with onions, then herring and carrots. (Adding carrots is a Scandinavian method and, although optional, it makes a prettier jar as well as adding nutritional value.) Top each layer with one quarter of the seasonings. There should be four layers. Add the pickling liquid to cover the layered ingredients and cover contents tightly. Allow to remain in refrigerator three or four days before serving.

8 servings

Plum Jam

plums
fructose
lemon juice, optional

Wash plums and remove pits. Simmer in a stainless steel or enameled pot until tender. Force through a coarse strainer and measure. For each cup of plum pulp, add ½ cup of fructose and, if you like, 2 tsps. lemon juice. Cook until thick on low heat, stirring frequently to prevent scorching. Store in sterilized jars. Allow to cool before sealing.

Spicy Plum-Apple Butter

2 cups plums, pitted
2 cups cooking apples, sliced
1½ cups fructose (more or less depending upon tartness of fruit and individual taste.)
1 tsp. cinnamon
¼ tsp. nutmeg
½ tsp. allspice
½ tsp. ground cloves

In a stainless steel or enameled saucepan, cook plums and apples at low heat until tender, about 15 minutes. Add small amount of water, if necessary. Press through coarse sieve. Reheat with fructose over low heat. Add spices. Cook until mixture sheets from the spoon. Place in sterilized jars. Allow to cool before covering with melted paraffin.

1½ pints

Pickles and Preserves

Spiced Apricot Jam

apricots
cinnamon
nutmeg
fructose

Wash apricots. Remove pits. Simmer in a stainless steel or enameled pot until soft. Force through a coarse strainer and measure. For each two cups of pulp add 1 teaspoon cinnamon, ½ tsp. nutmeg and ¾ cup fructose. Return to pot and cook until thick over low heat stirring frequently to prevent scorching. Place in sterilized jars, allow to cool and seal.

Apricot-Lime Marmalade

apricots
limes
fructose

Prepare apricot pulp as described in Spiced Apricot Jam, above. For each 2 cups of pulp add the juice and chopped rind of 1 lime (about ¼ cup each) and 1 cup fructose. Return to stainless steel kettle and simmer until thick, stirring frequently. Place in sterilized jars and seal.

Cherry-Pineapple Marmalade

1½ cups pineapple chunks
4 cups cherries
1½ cups fructose
¼ cup lemon juice

Wash cherries. Remove stems and pits. Coarsely chop the pineapple chunks and cherries. Place in a stainless steel kettle, stir in the fructose and let stand for at least 4 hours, not longer than 8 hours. Bring to a boil and let simmer until thick and clear, removing scum if necessary. Add lemon juice. Bring to a boil and simmer 3 minutes. Place in sterilized jar and seal.

2 pints

Pickled Watermelon Rind

2 lbs. watermelon rind
4 cups fructose
2 cups vinegar
1 cup water
1 tsp. cloves
1 tsp. allspice
1 stick cinnamon

Peel the green from the watermelon rind and cut into one-inch pieces. Let soak overnight in salted water. Drain and rinse thoroughly. Simmer for 5 minutes in boiling water. Make a syrup combining the fructose, vinegar, water and spices. With a slotted spoon remove the watermelon rind from the water and place in the pickling mixture. Bring to a boil once more and pack in sterile jars covering the rind with the syrup.

about 2 quarts

Minted Watermelon Rind

In the above recipe substitute 1 cup strong mint tea for the cup of water.

Anise Flavored Watermelon Rind

Add one star anise to each pint of pickled watermelon rind.

Suppliers of Fructose

If you are unable to obtain fructose from your grocer or health food store, write to one of the following American suppliers:

Batter-Lite Foods, Inc.
P.O. Box 341
Beloit, Wisconsin 53511

Doctor's Choice Fructose
Thompson Medical Co.
919 Third Avenue
New York, New York 10022

Estee Corporation
169 Lackawanna Avenue
Parsippany, New Jersey 07054

General Nutrition Corporation
921 Penn Avenue
Pittsburgh, Pennsylvania 15230

Or for your convenience, you may order fructose directly from the publisher in the following quantities:

1 lb. fructose in a pouch $5.95
2 lbs. fructose in a reusable canister $8.95
5 lbs. fructose in a bag $16.95

All prices include $2.00 postage and handling.

Send your check to:
Fructose/East Woods Press
820 East Boulevard
Charlotte, NC 28203

Alphabetical Index

The Fructose Cookbook

126

Index

127

About the Author

Minuha Cannon is a free-lance writer living in California. She is a former piano instructor and teacher of mentally handicapped children. When she isn't writing or cooking for a house full of guests, she is painting, playing the concertina or folk dancing.

The Fructose Cookbook grew out of Minu's interest in biochemestry and the healthy aspects of fructose. After some years of experimenting with fructose in her own repertoire of unusual, wholesome dishes, she was encouraged by friends to write this book. Her recipes tell the rest.

Minuha Cannon